Even in Winter

Jim Wilson

Even in Winter

Copyright © Jim Wilson 2015
Sebastopol, California
U.S.A.

All rights reserved.

ISBN: 9781514224649

Address all inquiries to:

jimfw@hotmail.com

or

Jim Wilson
P.O. Box 2756
Sebastopol, CA 95472

Table of Contents

Note: Many of the poems are untitled. If a poem has a title the Table of Contents uses the title. If the poem does not have a title, the Table of Contents uses the first line of the poem.

Poem	Page
Elbow Lake, Wisconson	8
Summerscape	9
Rain	10
Rain	11
Pond	12
Both/And	13
Sky	14
Cool	15
News	16
Daymare	17
Precognition	18
Summercape	19
Destination	20
Morning	21
Evaporation	22
Don't	23
Web	24
Wine	25
Sex	26
Day	27
Separation from the World	28
Corrective Lens	29
Ultimate Otherness	30
Turn	31

Poem	Page
Summerscape	32
Introductions	33
Songs	34
Friends	35
The Messenger	36
Lake	37
Last Night's Rain	38
Time	39
Companions	40
Slow	41
Past Present	42
For Jane and Werner	43
Climate Change	44
Piercing the Veil	45
Modernity	46
Cool	47
Rain	48
Rain	49
Damp	50
Bright	51
Scone	52
Rain	53
Cold	54
Rain	55
Wind	56
Cool	57
Night	58
Dusk	59
Naturescape	60
Warm Day	61
Sunlight	62

Poem	Page
Degrees	63
Asceticism	64
Even in Winter	65
Cars	66
Frost	67
A Merchant's View	68
Mist	69
Ghosts	70
Askew	71
Trees	72
Oaks	73
Kotodama	74
Dark	75
The Snowfall of Time	76
For a Deceased Lover	77
Rain	78
Moon	79
Futurescape	80
Renunciation	81
Lunch	82
Sun	83
Fog	84
Light	85
Sequence	86
Stars	87
Third Month	88
Recollection	89
Spring	90
Clouds	91
Routines	92
Springscape	93

Poem	Page
Exultation	94
The Weave of Time	95
I'm Caught	96
Free Verse Mind	97
Geek Poetry	98
Embodied	99
Embodied	100
Archaeology	101
Light	102
Gray	103
Dawn	104
Choirs	105
The Gift	106
Ordinary Time	107
Waves	108
Return	109
Afterthoughts	112
Other Books by the Author	118
About the Author	119

Even in Winter

Even in Winter

Elbow Lake, Wisconsin

Lake
Summer
Warm sunlight
A cautious deer
Deciduous trees
The sound of rustling leaves
As a camper makes his way
A few squirrels skitter away
Insects are dancing in the sun's rays
Thoughts settle and the mind is free from haze
There's some slight stirring from a few lazy waves
A truck in the distance filled with bundles of hay

Summerscape

Peace
Dawn
Silence
Solitude
A late summer sky
There is no wind stirring the trees
A few leaves have changed color and the long grass is dry

Even in Winter

Rain
Steady
All morning
The silent house
The silence within
Lake a path through the woods
That leads to a stream-fed pond,
A pond that's reflecting the sky

Rain
Late June
Afternoon
The waiting room
Insurance questions
Insurance benefits
It's complex and confusing
Old people waiting patiently
Documents are held in their hands
Filled out with all the proper numbers
Signs on the way to the final slumber

Pond

Breakfast
In the morning
Sunlight
Through the windows
The sound of the roses
Delays my plans
I stretch my arms and yawn
I decide to take a day off
They don't need me at work
I absent myself from the web
(I fondly recall some friends who are dead)
And listen to the wind instead
While I fold my clean clothes and make my bed
On the branch of the oak a sparrow has landed –
We speak to each other before he goes

Both/And

Hot
Clear sky
Afternoon
Early July
Under the oak trees
There are pools of cool shade
And the sound of rustling leaves
By a pathway hard to see
Fragments of songs that quickly fade,
Voices of friends who long ago strayed,
Indiscretions for which we both have paid
Are landmarks left behind as I walk the way
That end in the silence and stillness of a glade
By the river that's night, by the river that's day

Even in Winter

Sky
Grey
Morning
Subdued tones
Coffee and a scone
The July field littered with stones
The song of a bird blends with the ring of my cell phone

Cool
Monday
A gray sky
Early July
The heat wave's ended
Time feels stalled, suspended,
There's news of another war,
News that I've often heard before,
That is what happens when we keep score,
It continues until we say, 'No more.'

News
T.V.
Reporting
Propaganda
Makes me uneasy
It's manipulation
It's not conversation
It's not information
It is about power
It is about struggle
It is all about fear
Inculcating constant fear
Encouraging a flood of tears
Encouraging plots of revenge
Clinging to the wheel of samsara
Casting our despair into tomorrow

Daymare

Summer
In the garden
Roses
Recollections
Meander like a stream
Through a landscape
Of scenes from the future,
Unlikely possibilities
That still seem attractive
Dissolved by the acid of now –

They are like corpses on a battlefield
In the heat of a cloudless sky
Upon which numberless scavengers feed,
Messengers from the demon of the wheel of time –

White petals sway under the crows' black wings

Precognition

Hate
Anger
Enmity
Another war –
"We must save the earth
And all that is of worth,
We must save the human race,
We're in danger of extinction."
When people say this I think they mean
That we might disappear without a trace,
You see, it's we who are in danger;
The earth, suspended in vast space,
Nested in the stars' embrace,
Will not note our absence.

The full moon's presence
Shining on fields
Of melted glass
Stark silence
Angels weep
Ghosts pass
Winds dance
Sand

Summerscape

Leaves
Sky
Boulders
Afternoon
Warm wind moves the grass
A few swallows fly swiftly past

Tomorrow morning there'll be a Memorial Mass

Destination

Sorrow
Dirge
Our last words
At the graveside
While apple trees are in bloom –
Where do all of our friends and relatives go?
Under the warm cloudless afternoon sky there's no
trace of last winter's snow

Even in Winter

Morning
Cloudless
After the Mass
At the small coffee shop
I take a few moments to think and stop
As the grace of the brief Monday communion feels like fresh green grass
And touches my heart like a refreshing memory from childhood that sill nourishes me and does not pass

Evaporation

News
Voices
Odd choices
Propaganda
Editorials
It's kind of depressing
Noise gives rise to forgetting
Agitations are distressing –

It's better to take a long-term view,
It's better because it is less askew
When you comprehend that there is nothing new
And though these brief moments of peace and calm are few
They have the great virtue of ruthlessly cutting through
The cacophony of delusions that mask what is true

Even in Winter

Don't
Against
Refusal
To engage in
The madness of war;
War is not heroic,
It's better to be stoic
And remain aloof from all strife
Than to be the cause of more sorrow

Even in Winter

Web
Entice
Seduction
Stimulation

Hours in cyberspace
Feel sweet and exciting,
That's why it's so inviting
To follow the waves of desire,
To feed the mind and set it on fire
With just one click, that is all that's required

Even in Winter

Wine
Blind mind
Alcohol
Ethanol
Addiction
A cause of sin
A slippery slope
It is worse than dope
Alcohol leads to harm,
Harm to one's body and mind,
Harm to all of humankind,
Best to put alcohol behind
So that one can begin to feel whole –

Putting alcohol behind heals the soul

Even in Winter

Sex
Essence
Tendencies
Identity:
Is that what we are?
A bundle of desires?
Compelled by desires' fires?

Before we are born, where's the form?
And after we die where do we go?
Is it possible to contain the sky?

Even in Winter

Day
Or night
No windows
It's hard to say
With the changeless light
And the conditioned air
What nature offers today,
If the weather's nasty or fair.

It makes us think we're self-reliant,
It makes us brittle and uncompliant

Separation from the World

Vote
Or don't –
Elections
Candidates run
Making promises
Seeking our attention
For the campaign's duration
But the words have little meaning
And commitments are soon forgotten;
I'd rather stay home with Bible reading

Corrective Lens

Views
Constructs
Perspectives
Commentaries
Interpretations –

We do not see the world,
What we see is our own mind,
We see ev'rything through glasses
That distort all the things that we find
As if orange was the color of glasses,
Like those who believe that nothing surpasses
Their desires that crumble like broken fences,
As if a solid mountain range contained passes,
As if truth was determined by vote of the masses,
Or those who believe that the only thing we can grasp is
That which can be measured and observed by the five senses
Unconcerned and unaware that all these things become ashes
But all becomes clear when we think of this: ev'rything vanishes

Ultimate Otherness

Evening
Hot
Cloudless sky
A half-full moon,
A moon on the waning side,
Nonchalantly past the stars it slowly glides –

A thick thought of anger and revenge emerges in my mind and collides
With that transcendental compassion and all-embracing love I have thoroughly studied and hoped to internalize,
Hoping to grasp and hold them like the end of a race when one gets a prize,
Only to see it dissolve before one's eyes –

Kyrie Eleison
A pray'r, a sigh
Spacious sky
Dawn
Mercy

Even in Winter

Turn
Away
From the world
The world of strife
The world of sorrow
The world of contention
There's nothing worth killing for
Turn within and find the door
That leads to enduring peace
A blessedness that does not cease
The source of all that is good and true
Found in a land whose language is silence

Summerscape

Summer
Warm
August days
The morning haze
Drifting in from the sea stays
Until about eight or nine when the sun's rays
Evaporates the last traces of cool creating distinct
pools of shade
Cast by scattered old oak trees in my neighbor's dry
field while in the sky a few swift-moving clouds are
in beauty arrayed

Introductions

Eyes
Faces
Expressions
First impressions
A friend of a friend
At a lunchtime session
Perhaps two will become three
Though the future is hard to see
It has all the signs of a good start,
The conversation is flowing freely

Even in Winter

Songs
Folk songs
Melodies
And lines that rhyme
Songs of love and loss
Songs of celebration
Sung at the change of seasons
Marking the path the sun travels
In a galaxy of countless stars
In a vastness of countless galaxies . . .

Friends
Chairs
Table
Shared fables
Banter back and forth
Jokes about all of our foibles

The Messenger

Songs
Rhythms
Melodies
Cyclic seasons,
Cycles of the moon,
Cycles of precession,
Cycles I'm unaware of . . .

A few clouds in the sky above
On the maple tree there's a white dove
The sun in the sky is slightly past noon

Gabriel appears and speaks to me of love

Even in Winter

Lake
Moonlight
Reflected
Some ancient oaks
The sound of an owl
A quiet fox trots by
A camper sits by a fire
An angel touches the water
Ripples of dreams rustle some branches
Ripples of time as some sparks climb higher

Last Night's Rain

Rain
Ninth month
Before dawn
The rain ceases
Dawn light increases
The sound of falling drops
From the branches of the trees
Landing on the discarded leaves
Like the countless memories that leave
After I have had enough time to grieve

Even in Winter

Time
Money
Day and night
They slip away
But so do boulders,
So do mountain ranges,
Things are subject to changes,
Abandoned cars in a junkyard,
An old message on a greeting card,
A di'mond she decided to discard

Companions

Gray
Diffuse
September
The morning light
At the coffee shop
Fills the space with quiet.
Three friends sit at a table,
I think they are in their sixties,
They're relaxed, obviously at ease,
Like the stillness found in an autumn breeze.

Even in Winter

Slow
Ninth Month
Afternoon
It's not too hot
The nights are longer
My morning walk's colder
And sunrise sounds quieter,
I hear the call of solitude
The trees across the street have turned red
I think about something that Jesus said
Knowing that my friends wouldn't give it much cred,
Yet this is where I am, this is where I've been led,
All fear has vanished and there is not a trace of dread
As I contemplate what it means to be among the dead

Past Present

Dusk
Cool shade
September
Arthritis
Scattering leaves
I begin to grieve
In a way that's quiet,
For those whom I have loved,
For those who have passed away
I conjure our yesterdays
As the present swiftly fades
I walk once again with my friends –

There is a bridge formed by the mind,
On it the past and present combine,
Suspended over the chasm of time

Even in Winter

For Jane and Werner

Warm
Tenth month
Lots of sun
Summer lingers
A clear blue sky
I think about Jane
I think about Werner
I wonder how they're doing
In the small town of Gualala
On the coast of California
The waves of the ocean ebb and flow
Like memories of friends I used to know,
Like a quiet sunset that is nature's show –

I first met Jane and Werner thirty years ago

Climate Change

Hot
Strange days
It's too hot
For October
The days should be cool
But we will have to wait
For the first autumn wind,
For regular seasons to rule,
For human beings to step aside,
For people to withdraw like an ebb tide

Piercing the Veil

Warmth
Fall
No mist
October
Yet summer lingers
An old song on the radio
While I am having a scone and a cup of coffee –
Slowly I turn on the stream of time and I see my
friend with whom I danced long ago

Modernity

Sun
Tenth month
Clear morning
Anxiety
For humanity
Lost in a fog of greed,
Lost in gathering darkness,
Lost in the thrill of destruction,
Lost in a thicket of possessions,
Lost forever on the samsaric sea . . .

Even in Winter

Cool
Gray sky
October
The hot spell ends
It's autumn again
I hear another song
A melody that is long,
That resembles an endless dawn,
An intimacy that is close, not far,
Like the counterpoint of the distant stars

Even in Winter

Rain
Tenth month
Finally
The heat wave ends
It is cool again –
Every now and then
I'm able to see the light,
I let go of all that I know,
I step beyond the stream of feelings
Into a land beyond hope and fear
And sometimes a bright calmness appears,
A serenity banishing turmoil,
Like steam dispersing when a kettle boils,
Like falling rain in the tenth month of the year
Dispersing the heat and dust so the sky is clear

Even in Winter

Rain
Tenth month
On the streets
Fender benders
It happens each fall
People will not slow down
They do not want to recall,
Or they've important things to do,
So they just plow their way through the storm,
Though they cannot see where they are going,
Assuming their pace will always be the norm,
Until they meet an obstacle and come to harm.

Even in Winter

Damp
Sixth day
Of the week
It rained last night
The streets are still wet
Folks are out and about
Driving their cars to the stores
Holding their lists of things to get
Smiling at friends they have met by chance –
It is all a part of the human dance

Even in Winter

Bright
Tenth month
Morning light
Fall is quiet
There are fewer birds
There is less to be heard
Activities fall away
A brief wind and the maples sway
It's comforting watching children play
Sitting on a park bench day after day
It's easy to count the remaining days
Sitting on a park bench that an old friend made
Sitting on a park bench watching the seasons fade

For Rob and Stuart

Scone
Tenth month
Fall morning
Warm coffee
My mind wanders
I ponder friendship
I think about Rob
I think about Stuart
I think about loyalty
I think about anxiety
And about their generosity
I think about vulnerability
And about how kind they have been to me

Even in Winter

Rain
Tenth month
The last day
Of October
The rain is steady
The sound of the wipers
As I drive down the highway
As election day approaches
A surprising equanimity
Within and without encompasses me

Even in Winter

2013-10-31

Cold
Late fall
Morning sun
The house is quiet
My mother's birthday
The last day of the month
The last day of October
Sometimes in my dreams I see her
She looks happy, without much to say,
Gathered with others who have passed away

Redemption

Rain
Late fall
November
It rained all night
Mist and dreams remain

When I look at my life
I feel like a survivor.
I've outlived those I have loved.
In more than a few cases
Only I remember places
Or the features of those faces
That have left only a few traces.

Redwood trees once covered endless acres
And passenger pigeons once filled the sky,
Beaches are reshaped by persistent breakers
And nations vanish no matter how hard we try
To hold back the tide of impermanence. We sigh.

This is the nature of the world in which we live.
All our activity takes place upon a sieve
That holds a form for just a moment and then gives
It back into the river of eternal time.

"All is vanity," thus speaks Ecclesiastes.
This is the conclusion from those who truly see.
But Ecclesiastes has something else to say,
To love God who dwells beyond night, dwells beyond day,
And follow his commandments until one's dying day.

Even in Winter

Wind
Leaves fall
Late morning
November cool
The sound of traffic
Sunlight from a clear sky

I should visit the river.
It is a good meditation
To watch the ever-moving water,
To watch the leaves drift by on the currents,
Currents which will carry them to the ocean

Even in Winter

Cool
Morning
Saturday
November light

What do dreams mean?
Are they other worlds?
Some are realistic,
Others are fantastic.
Some dreams tell a story
While others just set a scene.
Perhaps they are biological
Even when they are illogical.

I do not know what my dreams will bring,
I do not know what will happen today,
I do not know what song my neighbor will sing
Or when I have lunch with my friend what he will say.
The world we live in is a mysterious place,
Things are here and then they vanish without a trace,
Like a dream whose contours I cannot remember,
Or how the moon looked on the twelfth of November.

Walking, dreaming, coming, and going is the way,
Though appearances make us think that we will stay
We are just visitors into the realm of dreams
Walking across a bridge that is also a stream

Even in Winter

Night
Sleepless
Aching joints
The full moon's glow
Interrupted dreams
November silence
Restless recollections
Nothing too terrible:
The persistence of debt,
The ambiance of regrets,
Obligations I have not met,
Those times I wasn't very kind
(I had other things on my mind)
So that friendships withered away
Like a field of harvested hay
That's turned to stubble and exposed clay –

The sunrise has been endlessly delayed

Even in Winter

Dusk
Full moon
November
Cloudless sky
The air is cool
The traffic's slowing down
No customers in the store
There is a park two blocks away
With a year-round creek running through it,
A grove of redwood trees stands beside it,
I can hear their shadows slowly growing,
I can sense the world of dreams reforming

Naturescape

Clear
Starlight
Before dawn
November cold
The moon has gone down
The sound of my footsteps
There is no wind this morning
The Orion constellation,
Like an adagio for my eyes,
Sends me an invitation to the sky

Even in Winter

Warm day
Fall
Afternoon
November dry
I'm thinking about regrets
They resemble clouds that are nailed to the sky,
Or a decrepit wooden fence that has needed repair for a long time,
Or a concrete barrier that has been set –

The past does not disappear
Fear of fossils
Fear of sand
Dust
Deserts

Even in Winter

Sunlight
Cold
November
A few strangers
Memories like leaves scatter
Is that me in the picture from years ago?
I used to believe that there were many intriguing
things that I could know –

Having entered the roaring blizzard of silence and
endlessness the pursuit of knowledge became a greed
to forgo,
In the middle of a field whose perimeters are only
vaguely perceived, in the shade cast from a massive
boulder dropped by an ancient glacier, there lies a
small patch of slowly melting snow

Degrees
Schools
Studying
Education
Gaining more and more knowledge,
After all, that is why we go to college.
Yet all of this information takes us step by eager step
to the edge
Of annihilation. It is as if we are standing with a
great wind behind us which is the cyclone of
knowledge
And this cyclone seeks to maliciously tear us from our
safe ledge –

The ledge felt small, like a garden with a hedge,
But a garden is a realm,
It is enough
For a life –

Peace
With God

Asceticism

Fog
Morning
Thick and cold
November gray
Renunciation
That's a difficult word
One that is not often heard
Lack of things means you've not prospered,
That abundance has been deferred,
Perhaps some tragedy has occurred,
There must be some kind of explanation;
An ongoing rationalization
For a psychological repression?
That it's attractive is beyond conception,
It can't be *voluntary* renunciation.

There is beauty in the sight of a leafless tree,
A distant solo flute's exquisite melody,
In a room a single book that is often read,
A few words overheard that a stranger once said,
A walk along the beach when the ocean is calm,
The transcendental presence that glows in a Psalm
That opens a door that allows us to perceive
Waves of vast spaciousness from a limitless sea

Even in Winter

Cold
Freezing
December
Frost on the ground
A cloudless sunrise
The sound of the furnace
There are tasks I have to do
Projects that I need to finish
Reluctantly I relinquish
The pause that I place after prayer
Yet a certain stillness stays with me
As I walk past a familiar oak tree

Even in Winter

Cars
Traffic
Holiday
Destinations
People on their way
Visiting Mom and Dad
Because they live far away
So it is difficult to say
How they are doing as they grow old,
Mom, especially, is tending to fade

Even in Winter

Frost
Cold fields
December
I had some dreams
I don't remember
The specific details.
A lot of things are like that.
The first time I forgot the date
Of a lover who had passed away
(Realizing this after a few days)
I felt like I had been given a simple task
And then failed to follow through on my assignment,
Kind of like when you forget to do your homework
And then the teacher calls on you for no reason.
But I digress, a tendency of the season.
Events fall into the swirling fog of the past
Like a dream I had last night which cannot be grasped,
Like a melody whose last cadence has ended,
Like a great cause which is no longer defended,
Or a popular song that is no longer sung,
A mountain temple bell that is no longer rung –

Into the ocean of silence all things return,
Into the great mystery from which they were born.

A Merchant's View

Cold
Twelfth Month
Not too cold
Before Christmas
The stores are well stocked
At this time of the year
I always feel conflicted –
Part of me wants people to buy,
Part of me wants people to save,
To renounce all those things that they crave,
To leave the world behind with a sigh,
To live a life that's more restricted.
Sometimes, after a sale, I feel bad,
As a merchant you'd think I'd feel glad,
But this is the way the world is run,
People prefer material things,
People dislike winter and prefer spring,
Though the fate of all existing things
Resembles mountains that are vanishing
Into the emptiness from whence they came,
From this perspective all things are the same,
Like an empty mirror in a gilded frame.

But I have to turn away from all of these thoughts;
I offer a prayer for the customer who's bought
Much more than he needs, while in the large parking lot
A small choir reminds me of those angels on high
Singing praises to the stars, praises to the sky,
That once upon a time many centuries ago
Our Savior was born on a cold night filled with snow.

Even in Winter

Mist
Winter
Diffuse light
January
I'd like to tarry
But I have things to do
Before the day is through
So I set out for the store
There are many tasks, always more
Things to do like vacuuming the floor,
Washing the dishes from the day before

Even in Winter

Ghosts –

Time bends.
I see friends.
I can't pretend
That they are not there.
Those I've loved from the past
Are with me, they have not passed.
The present is not real to me;
It is only a fabrication
That hides our ultimate destination.

Askew

Dice
Chaos
Fortuna
A long nightmare
Sunrise in the west
A rose blooms in the snow
Traffic stops when it should go
A surrender ends in conquest
A beggar on the street knows what's best
A politician tells the truth in jest

Even in Winter

Trees
Branches
Without leaves
On sunny days
The air crisp and cold
With a blue sky behind
Have a skeletal presence
How long will the winter cold last?
They're tired of all the maneuverings,
Of all the motions and countermotions
Buried underneath the wind-blown drifts of snow
Hearts have lost the capacity for ebb and flow

Even in Winter

Oaks
First month
Bare branches
By the driveway
It's quiet and still
There's a warmth in my soul
Sunlight strikes the window sill,
I take another prescribed pill,
From behind the clouds the sky is blue,
That's not a surprise, it's something I knew,
Though I forget when I have a lot to do,
My life's coming to a close, it is almost through.

Kotodama

Frost
Dawn
Cold walk
Slow morning
A golden sunrise
Then an unexpected surprise
When images and thoughts about my mother arise;
In particular I can recall the challenging look that would appear in her eyes
When someone would misuse a word my mother would sigh,
Lean forward and then she would try
To explain that words
Are alive,
Like thyme,
Oaks,
Grass . . .

Even in Winter

Dark
Darkness
A slow dawn
Overcast sky
Frosted rural fields
Slowly the darkness yields
The rural road is quiet
It's still too early for commerce
Not a trace of wind that I can feel
My friend has died but it doesn't seem real

The Snowfall of Time

Dawn
Slowly
Memories
From yesterday
From years that have passed
Memories of sunset
Memories of ocean waves
Memories of broken windows
Memories of long mountain shadows
Falling on accumulated sorrows

For a Deceased Lover

Friend
Lover
Years have passed
Frost on the grass
Has its brief presence
And then it's gone again.
But some things just disappear
Like those species from long ago
Sometimes uncovered in blocks of snow –

Frozen memories are all that I know.

Even in Winter

Rain
Steady
For three days,
There's more to come
(Mid-January)
Driving is more cautious
There's a reluctance to shop
Living becomes more domestic,
Do the laundry, empty the closet,
Chop onions and carrots for a slow stew

Even in Winter

Moon
Full moon
Winter moon
A cold, calm moon
January moon
Moonlight bleaches the sky
Ev'rything under the moon
(Trees, houses, boulders, flying owls)
Has taken on a silvery tinge –

The sound of the wind between the branches

Futurescape

Blue
Sunlight
A few clouds
The winter sky
Not a plane in sight
Parked cars gathering dust
After the great vanishing
The intersections are quiet
A pack of coyotes cross the street
The manicured gardens are unwatered

Renunciation

Time
Slow
Sunlight
Afternoon
February
A clear cloudless sky
The air is cold and dry
I am at peace in my room
In my silent hermitage
I sense the presence of God
The gentle touch of timelessness
Is so much more than I can grasp
I become inarticulate –

A coyote briefly trots by
A satellite is launched into space
Saturn is slowly turning direct
In Andromeda a new star is born
A sparrow appears on the windowsill
A new Buddhist Nun has her long hair shorn
An ocean wave becomes perfectly still

Even in Winter

Lunch
Winter
Holiday
MLK Day
At the greasy spoon
People in a good mood
(Some with friends, some with children)
Order their hamburgers with fries
While joking about their absent friends
And the latest political scandal

Even in Winter

Sun
Winter
A clear sky
Crisp and cold air
I've been sick for six days
This is my first day out
Running some basic errands
To test my stamina to see
The status of my recovery –

I drive to the beach to look at the sea

Even in Winter

Fog
Morning
A cold dawn
A fine stillness
I stifle a yawn
I am not really tired
A cup of tea is brewing
At the moment, nothing's required
Briefly the wind stirs, I feel inspired –

Deo Gratias, Deo Gratias

Even in Winter

Light
Shadows
The wind stirs
Mist drifts away
The sound of a bell
The first buds on the quince
Last night moonlight dimmed the stars
Last year a friend of mine fell
It was a slow recovery
Old age means you have to be careful
Blossoms in a steady wind will soon fall

Sequence

Quince
In bloom
The gray sky
Is persistent
It's inconsistent
The cold does not relent
Yet the bright blossoms are sent
As messengers that spring will come,
That the cold will, in a few weeks, end –

After the quince first the plum, then cherry,
Then fields of apple blossoms without end

Even in Winter

Stars
Cool air
The third month
Jupiter shines –

At a talk last night
The speaker spoke of God
And the transcending of time,
That there's an eternal spring
Found at the center of a field,
Whose waters are clear and refreshing,
That flows through memory and through dreams,
That flows through worlds both seen and unseen,
That speaks to us of the neverending

Even in Winter

Third month
Morning
A sunny sky
I saw Joan on youtube
She was exactly as I remembered;
Articulate, sweet, analytical, with those awesome
wide eyes

Recollection

Gray
Third month
Morning mist
Calalilies
Have started to bloom
I had a dream last night
I send a friend an email
The sound of a passing truck
Today's an anniversary,
It's the day my good friend passed away,
But that happened how many years ago?

Even in Winter

Spring
Morning
Trees budding
Calalilies –
Talking with neighbors
Over the just-clipped hedge,
They are thinking of planting
One of those Japanese maples
In their backyard so that they can see
The change of the colors that autumn brings,
And the bare-branched beauty that's found in winter,
And the birds after they return and begin to sing,
And the cooling shade that's needed in the summer heat,
And the soothing sound of rustling leaves in a summer breeze

Even in Winter

Clouds
Taurus
A chorus
Of bright flowers
Grown by my neighbors
That I get to savor
While I clean up the kitchen
I apuse and look out the window
On a landscape of good memories,
On a grove of gone friends whom I still know

Routines

Warm
Morning
The Fourth Month
Monday begins
The work week starts
I drive to the store
(My home away from home)
Dust the tables, sweep the floor,
I count the change in the draw'r,
I make myself a pot of tea,
Black tea, with caffeine, something hearty,
I turn on the lights and unlock the door

Springscape

Dawn
Night's gone
Mid-April
Light from the Psalms
The sound of the sky
Right now I think of you
Our years together were few
Bright lilies grow in the garden
A butterfly sips some drops of dew
Sprites sing by the stream a song that is new

Exultation

God
My Lord
My Refuge
My Salvation
How was I so blind
How was I so unkind
That I denied your presence,
That I denied your constant grace –

My life is brief and evanescent,
Yet Thou hast touched me and caressed my face;
I thought that all things vanished like stars in space,
But now I know that nothing ever really dies.

The Weave of Time

Paths
Choices
Destiny
April morning
Are we really free?
Decisions I have made,
Consequence I have weighed,
Seeds I have planted in the sand,
The future remains an unknown land,
A fabric made from the past's many strands.

Even in Winter

I'm caught,
Puzzled,
By two voices
Offering me choices:
The path of poetry's calling to me,
In contrast, there is the quiet path that leads to eternity.

Free Verse Mind

Words
Phrases
Poetry
Modernity
It's all about me
There's no community
Individuality
Is what we mean by being free
Which leads to sessions of therapy –

In an airless desert there are no trees

Geek Poetry

X
Y
Counting
Conforming
It is like a game
(Ev'ry game of chess is the same?)
Some people, I suspect, think that this is kind of lame,
Counting those syllables without any sense of shame,
But it's all good, no one's to blame –

It's not about fame,
It's about
Beauty
Shape
Form

Embodied

Poems
Songs
Rhythms
Clapping hands

The pulse of a band
Hawking wares from a sidewalk stand
An a capella choir sings praises to the sky
At a family gathering a newborn baby sometimes
giggles and sometimes cries

Embodied

Songs
Rhythms
Words that flow
Phrases that sing
Like blessings in spring,
Where did poetry go? –

It has lost its sense of time,
Poets seem to no longer know,
Poets seem to no longer feel,
Poets seem out of touch with the pulse
That gives words life, causing them to shimmer,
A spark that's dropped on the field of forever,
Like the cycle of beauty seasons deliver,
Like when your body feels the flow of a river

Archaeology

Soup
Rice
Spring rolls
Sweet and sour
The Chinese rest'rant
I take a break for an hour
I turn off the cell phone so it won't have the power
To disrupt my excavating a poem from an uncarved
block where it's trapped, where it glows

Even in Winter

Light
April
A bird trills
Morning coffee
I think about God,
I think about Love
And how He saved me
When I was lost at sea.
The utterly unworthy
Now have a way to be set free.
"I am the way, the truth, and the life,"
Is the way to the cessation of strife –

The sky today is open and spacious
The oak tree's shape is jagged and gracious
A few penstemons are blossoming
Our galaxy continues turning
A hummingbird briefly flutters
In the distance something hovers
Something ultimately other
Something beyond what I can sense
Something that's vast and immense
A pervasive presence
I am overwhelmed
I'm not at the helm
An hour has passed
A blade of grass
A warm wind stirs
Timelessness
Sparrows
Psalms

Even in Winter

Gray
April
No wind stirs
Easter morning
A Psalm's soothing words
The world's silent and still
I live on a rural road
There is no traffic this morning
I'm thinking about the empty tomb
In the distance the swift flight of a bird

Even in Winter

Dawn
And calm
Communion
"Take eat, take drink."
As the Lord asked
Some bread and a cup
A luminosity
An infusion from beyond
The gateway to the mystery
"Do this in remembrance of me."
A moment of surpassing beauty
A vastness greater than an endless sea

Even in Winter

Choirs
Voices
Angelic
Palestrina
Perfect counterpoint
Music that's God-inspired
'Kyrie Eleison'
And I enter another realm,
A realm where all sins are forgiven –

In the house of eternity I'll dwell

The Gift

Luck?
Karma?
Good fortune?
Circumstances?
My life has been blessed,
Blessed by loving parents,
Blessed by numerous good friends,
Blessed by dreams of peace and quiet

This is not something that I deserve,
It's a grace that I will seek to preserve

Ordinary Time

Warm
Morning
The fifth month
Monday errands
Commerce begins
Grocery shopping
Pay some bills online
Starbuck's good for a break
Pick up some prescriptions
The car needs an oil change
And then it's late afternoon
I go home, return to my room
I decide to not eat dinner
I contemplate the Psalm for the day
For some troubled friends I decide to pray
Its' been a good day bit it ends too soon
I fall asleep drenched in the light of the moon

Even in Winter

Waves
Warm sand
The Fifth Month
We are all lost
Trying to find peace
Or some satisfaction
But it's only inaction
When all our thoughts and strivings cease
(That's what it takes, that is the cost)
We open to the presence of grace
That is when all of our fears are released

Return

Thoughts
Morning
Dream warnings
And images
Vanish with the sun
The day has begun
I turn to the day's tasks
It's a housecleaning day
Which I find satisfying
Cleaning all of the dishes
Running the washer and dryer
Hanging up the clothes in order
Outside I trim the garden border
In the late afternoon it's time for tea
A voice from the dream realm returns to me,

"All of these things, ev'rything that you see
Resembles the sand cast up from the sea,
Shifting, changing, without stability,
Like smoke in the air, leaves falling from a tree,
This is their inevitable destiny,
They will soon be gone even from memory,
But there is one thing which never disappears,
It transcends all our sorrows, transcends all our fears,
Finding this realm means the cessation of all tears,
It is accessed through the door of the infinite heart;
Turning to the formless is how we begin, how we start,

It is the path of beauty from which we must not depart,
It is found in the stillness at the center of the storm,
It is found in the silence before anything was formed,
Before there was day, before there was night, before any thing
There exists the grace-filled song of silence that eternity sings."

Even in Winter

Afterthoughts

For those interested in the formal aspects of the poems in this collection, here are a few afterthoughts. I take a formal and syllabic approach to writing poetry. A formal syllabic approach means that the length of a line is predetermined by a formal structure based on the number of syllables in the line for that particular form. There are lots of syllabic forms these days in English language poetry. The forms used in this collection, and their syllable counts, are as follows:

The Etheree: 1-2-3-4-5-6-7-8-9-10
The Fibonacci: 1-1-2-3-5-8-13-21-34, etc.
The Lucas: 2-1-3-4-7-11-18, etc.
The Even Sequence: 2-2-4-6-10-16, etc.
100 Friends: 2-4-2-4-6-4-6-8-6-8-10-8-10-12-10

All of these forms share an overall shape: they start with very short lines of one or two syllables, or counts, and then gradually open up into longer count lines. Because they share this similar shape I thought they work well with each other. The shared overall shape gives the collection a sense of unity, while the variety of pacing as the poem moves to longer lines keeps the collection from becoming monotonous.

The Etheree

The simplest form is the Etheree. It is a ten line form and the count for each line simply follows that of counting from 1 to 10. The first line has one syllable, the second line has two, the third line three, etc., on up to the tenth line with ten syllables. Most of the poems in this collection are Etheree. Since discovering the form I have found it an attractive form and congenial for poetic expression.

Like other forms, Etheree poets have played with the Etheree form, creating variations on the basic formal structure. There is the reverse Etheree: 10-9-8-7-6-5-4-3-2-1. For some reason this variation has rarely attracted me, but I have seen it used fairly frequently.

And then there is the double Etheree: 1-2-3-4-5-6-7-8-9-10-(10)-9-8-7-6-5-4-3-2-1. I put one of the lines in parentheses (10), because some poets will use the 10 count line as a pivot, and have only one ten count line in a double Etheree, while others will repeat the ten count line.

There is also the extended Etheree which carries the count past the ten count line. In this variation the poet might go on to a twelfth line, which would have twelve syllables. Or to a fourteenth line, which would have fourteen syllables. This is a variation that I frequently use. It gives the poet the opportunity to continuing the form into longer lines.

Another variation for the Etheree is to linger over a particular line count. For example, a poet might have four lines of 4 count before going on to the 5 count line. This allows the poet to create a longer poem while still adhering to the basic structure of the Etheree. I think of this as a slow motion Etheree, because the pace with which the line count increases is halted at various points. I use this Slow Motion Etheree fairly often.

Etheree can be found on the following pages: 8, 10, 11, 13, 15, 16, 18, 22, 23, 24, 25, 26, 27, 28, 29, 31, 33, 34, 36, 37, 38, 39, 40, 41, 42, 43, 44, 46, 47, 48, 49, 50, 51, 52, 53, 54, 55, 56, 57, 58, 59, 60, 64, 65, 66, 67, 68, 69, 70, 71, 72, 73, 75, 76, 77, 78, 79, 80, 81, 82, 83, 84, 85, 86, 87, 89, 90, 91, 92, 83, 94, 95, 97, 100, 102, 103, 104, 105, 106, 107, 108, 109.

The Fibonacci

The Fibonacci has a small, but dedicated, following. There is at least one, online, journal devoted to the form. And you find examples of this form in unexpected places. For example, A. E. Stallings has four Fibonacci in her latest collection, *Olives*.

The form is based on the Fibonacci Sequence, a mathematical sequence of numbers that is based on an additive process. The sequence starts with the numbers 1, 1. 1 + 1 = 2, so the third line has 2 syllables. Then you add 2 to the previous number, 1, and that gets you 3. So the fourth line has three syllables. 3 + 2 = 5, so the fifth line has five counts. This procedure continues and you get an open ended sequence which begins: 1-1-2-3-5-8-13, etc. Most Fibonacci I have seen have six lines: 1-1-2-3-5-8, for a total of 20 syllables. But I have seen Fibonacci that move into the longer count lines.

As in the Etheree, Fibonacci poets will sometimes write a poem with a reversed count: 8-5-3-2-1-1. Or a Double Fibonacci: 1-1-2-3-5-8-(8)-5-3-2-1-1.

Fibonacci can be found on the following pages: 9, 14, 19, 35, 45, 74, 98, 99, and 101.

The Lucas

The Lucas is similar to the Fibonacci but the first two numbers in the sequence differ from the better known Fibonacci. The first two numbers of the Lucas Sequence are 2, 1. Using the same additive procedure as in the Fibonacci, the syllable counts for the Lucas lines are as follows: 2-1-3-4-7-11-18, etc.

Lucas can be found on the following pages: 20, 30, 32, 61, 62, and 63.

The Even Sequence

The Even Sequence follows the same procedures to generate the syllable count for the lines of the poem as does the Fibonacci and the Lucas. But the first two numbers for the Even Sequence are 2, 2. Using the same additive procedure as in the Fibonacci, the syllable counts for the Even Sequence lines are as follows: 2-2-4-6-10-16, etc.

Even Sequence can be found on the following pages: 21, 88, and 96.

100 Friends

This is a form I created. A collection of 100 Friends poems can be found in my previously published collection *Safe Harbor*. The form has fifteen lines with syllable counts as follows: 2-4-2-4-6-4-6-8-6-8-10-8-10-12-10. The overall count is 100 syllables which gave rise to the name of the form.

100 Friends can be found on the following pages: 12 and 17.

The Very Short Line

All of these forms begin with very short lines. I define a very short line as a line of 4 syllables or less. The very short line is a challenge to the poet. It is surprising how many syllabic forms begin with very short lines. These include Cinquain, Lanterne (which consists entirely of very short lines), and all of the forms used in this collection.

My approach to the very short line has been to use a list approach to this feature. A list of items, often for shopping, contains information in a succinct form. I have tended to use the opening very short lines to offer a seasonal and/or temporal reference. Names of months are good; and if you substitute Tenth Month for October, you get a shorter count. Seasonal names (spring, summer, fall, winter) all fall into the short count limitation and provide a lot of information. The time of day is also available: dawn, day, dusk, night, etc. Lunar phases are a good resource for the very short line: full moon, new moon, etc. Weather based phenomena are also good words for setting the scene: rain, fog, mist, dust, hot, cold, frost, ice, warm, wind, etc.

I have been influenced in this approach by Japanese poetry. In that tradition setting the season is a significant task for the poet and I found I could carry over this focus by using the very short line to give a general impression of the season and/or time of the year/day.

For those who are interested in how to construct a very short line I would like to suggest two resources: the poets Samuel Menashe and Jane Reichhold. Menashe was a minimalist metric poet of great skill. Though his lines are very short, they often encompass entire thoughts. Jane Reichhold is a haiku poet of prolific output and amazing skill. I would recommend getting her *A Dictionary of Haiku, Second Edition*. Reichhold takes a free verse approach to lineation. Her skill at shaping a very short line so that it is meaningful without becoming anorexic has been a major influence on my own writing. I recommend her work, and this book in particular, for anyone who is composing in syllabic forms that use very short lines. The craft of shaping those lines is so skillfully and beautifully demonstrated in this collection of haiku, and done in such an inviting way, that I think it will open many doors for others.

Other Books by the Author

Safe Harbor
A collection of Etheree, Fibonacci, and 100 Friends poems.
ISBN: 9781482551983
$12.00

Lanterne Light
Contains Lanternes, Tetractys, and Cinquain
ISBN: 9781484880944
$12.00

A Night of Many Sonnets
Sonnets, Sestinas, and Interlocks
ISBN: 9781503240391
$14.95

Shorter Haiku Journeys
Haiku Sequences
ISBN: 9781507568255
$9.00

Tanka River
Tanka Sequences
ISBN: 978-1490550756
$12.00

Microcosmos
Renga
ISBN: 9781492933229
$26.95

About the Author

The author has travelled widely including Korea, Japan and Poland. He studied Buddhism in East Asia and the U.S. He has worked in a variety of occupations from Alaska to Arizona. He has a longstanding interest in poetry, philosophy, spirituality, and music. He currently works as the manager of a local book and tea store in Northern California and is a member of a local Quaker Meeting.

The author may be contacted at:

jimfw@hotmail.com

When contacting the author by email please put in the subject line 'author inquiry', so that the author can spot it.

Made in the USA
San Bernardino, CA
27 October 2016